In the Muddy Shoes of Morning

In the Muddy Shoes of Morning

John B. Lee

Hidden Brook Press

First Edition

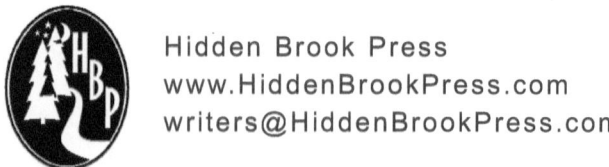

Hidden Brook Press
www.HiddenBrookPress.com
writers@HiddenBrookPress.com

Copyright © 2010 Book – Hidden Brook Press
Copyright © 2010 Poetry – John B. Lee

All rights for poems revert to the author. All rights for book, layout and design remain with Hidden Brook Press. No part of this book may be reproduced except by a reviewer who may quote brief passages in a review. The use of any part of this publication reproduced, transmitted in any form or by any means, electronic, mechanical, photocopied, recorded or otherwise stored in a retrieval system without prior written consent of the publisher is an infringement of the copyright law.

In the Muddy Shoes of Morning
by John B. Lee

Cover Design – Richard M. Grove
Cover Photograph – Richard M. Grove
Layout and Design – Richard M. Grove

Typeset in Garamond

Printed and bound in Canada

Library and Archives Canada Cataloguing in Publication

Lee, John B., 1951-
    In the muddy shoes of morning / John B. Lee.

Poems.
ISBN 978-1-897475-64-5 = 19781897475645

    I. Title.

PS8573.E348I523 2010   C811'.54   C2010-907325-8

to Cathy

Acknowledgements

Poems from *In the Muddy Shoes of Morning* have appeared in:

And Left a Place to Stand On, Baby Boomer, Ellipsis, Kohinoor, Petra Kenney Award pamphlet, Poemata, Poetry Café, Saving Banister, Vallum, The Voice, Tough Times: when the money doesn't love us, Voices Israel, and *Windsor Review*

"In the Same Breath" won the 2009 *Cranberry Tree Press Award*

"The Fishgutters in the Morning" won first place in the *Canadian Poetry Association's Annual poetry Award in 2009*

"In the Muddy Shoes of Morning" was sole Canadian recipient of the *Petra Kenney Poetry Prize* in 2009

"The Last Resting" was set to music and performed as part of *Dancing on Summer Strings*, a contemporary dance and poetry performance of Theatre London

Table of Contents

Strange Beautiful

The Fishgutters in the Morning – *p. 3*
Strange Beautiful – *p. 5*
The Hobbyist – *p. 7*
Two Good Men Having a Conversation – *p. 9*
Failing Russian – *p. 10*
A Small Unquiet War – *p. 12*
Opossum in the Barbecue – *p. 14*
To Live the Day that Honours God
    We Must Love the Dust We're Born From – *p. 16*
Look at That – *p. 18*
Observation Through a Wind-Stirred Tree – *p. 19*
Slow Smoke – *p. 21*
Again – *p. 22*
Inside the Light – *p. 23*
Being Seen – *p. 24*
Let it Go – *p. 26*
The Children Come – *p. 29*
This Listening – *p. 31*
Imaginary Solitude – *p. 32*

The Silver-Lake Suite

Being Where We Are – *p. 37*
Finding a Used Condom on the Lynn River Trail – *p. 38*
Thirteen Turtles – *p. 40*
General Impression Size and Shape – *p. 41*
Whooping Crane, Silver Lake – *p. 43*
The Turtle Mother – *p. 45*
Watching TV – *p. 47*
The Saddening Green – *p. 49*
Coneflower Meadow, Silver Lake, Summer 2010 – *p. 51*
Knowing My World – *p. 52*

Strange Blueberries

In the Muddy Shoes of Morning – *p. 59*
Strange Blueberries – *p. 61*
The Lengthening Ash – *p. 62*
Watching Purple Martens Glean
      Mayflies from the Wind – *p. 64*
The Weakening – *p. 66*
The Starving Man and I – *p. 68*
When the Light Returns – *p. 70*
Heat Lightning – *p. 71*
Teaching My Dog to Read:
      The First Lesson – *p. 73*
Cozy – *p. 74*
Remembering the Moment Yet to Come – *p. 75*
Pokeweed – *p. 77*
Behold the Child of Time – *p. 79*
The Appetite's Result – *p. 80*
What Falls on the Hill Doesn't Love Me – *p. 81*
A Stone on the Wind – *p. 82*
In the Same Breath – *p. 83*
I am a Work of Art Do Not Touch Me – *p. 84*
Meditations on a Fly in Church – *p. 85*

The Darkness Within

Learning the Dead Man's Float – *p. 89*
The Darkness Within – *p. 91*
The Last Resting – *p. 92*
A Rising Stillness – *p. 93*
Flight School – *p. 95*
Ill Beauty – *p. 97*
Angel House – *p. 99*
Toward the Horses – *p. 100*
Vantage – *p. 102*

A Note About the Author – *p. 105*

Strange Beautiful

The Fishgutters in the Morning

I have seen them
taking their ease
some of them leaning
on the cinderblock wall
some of them
sitting on ledges
or resting on gravel
their low voices smouldering
their quick hands
withering like candlewick
and all of them knifeless
in this
all of them here
and taken away from
the sharp skill of their work
and even the men
are skeined in hairnets, heads caught
like the walked-through weave
of old barn cobwebs

and I imagine
them turning the doomed
scale-skinned harvest
and remember
a Chinese story from childhood
where the fisherman
found himself blessed by three wishes
when the fish in his hands
begged for its life
in a dream-water voice

and I think also
of old Santiago
his damaged hands
his marlin vanishing
in the shark belly of a blue-eyed sea

and I think of how I once watched
a woman
cleaning the smelt
with uncle up to his knees
in quicksilver spawn of moonlight
and I wonder was it my mother
was it me
at the table
a thousand spines on my plate
fine as watch springs
made for the measuring
of broken time

Strange Beautiful

On the deck
of the Port Dover
Fishing Museum
men are working
one with a grinder
one with a wire brush
both rubbing rust from the red-black railing
and I pause
in the noise and notice
within the belly of a hollowed out
iron sculpture of a fish suspended as if swimming
a nest
containing two open-mouthed
robin fledglings
and I
stop
in the loud rasp
of worker's wheel and brush bristle
to watch
life swallowed in its thatched circumference
like an old dark-strawed garden hat
eaten by
ancient ichthyology
that small leviathan
that living worm-want baited by birds

the man with the brush
tells me
when the mother comes
she flies in
at the mouth
like a meal
and she worries her wings
as birds do dying
she flutters against danger
and feeds her sky-startled young
waiting in the rain-eaten
oxidation
of this ferruginous fish
cleaned to the bone by
the fire in which it was forged
while the gut-red
rust of the world
weeps in wet weather
"and soon they'll be gone"
he says
though the man
with the grinder
never stops working
he's kneeling into the noise
as if he were praying, he shouts
about birds at a world gone deaf
in his hands

The Hobbyist

The thin white-haired elder walks an otherwise empty beach
cripple-armed by the conjoined cane
of his metal detector
sweeping the sand
for change
he chases blind coin
pausing with the manufactured interest
of a dull-man's morning
he stoops and digs, stoops and digs
sifts the copper and rust
in the penny-light of brown earth's deep ecru
looking for lost gold
the accidental el dorado
of a loose-fingered bride
the delicate necklace of a weeping child
someone else's coffee and cream
he wears a headset
listens to the sad clink of a fire-bent spike
for the half-burnt match-wither of a ruined nail
held in the porridge well
of the water line
here where soft islands
mark low tide

he stops, he stands
he shakes his dross
he sounds the stones he sees
looking for worth in the luckless rattle
of a gambler's hopeless cup
wondering perhaps if here among pebbles
he might find himself
in the God-tossed day
in this divine tedium
of unfound things
where gull feathers stray
and dog sticks drift
and cracked shells grind green glass

Two Good Men Having a Conversation
for Bill Ehrhart

Quite simply: two good men conversing
well fed and prosperous
we walked the beautiful summer-blue
pax aqua of Port Dover
and you having seen a documentary
on the history of genocide
how even old-testament Jehovah
favoured the massacre of multitudes
think of the great diluvial wash of the drowned
the 'everyone everywhere' sunk upon mountains
beyond gopher-wood cubits
their skulls like underwater knocking together of stones
think of the terrible conflagration of cities
the ashen immolation of Gomorrah
those flickering faces like the sneer of horses burned in barn fires
or ancient Jericho doomed by the stilling of one small star
and you the father of daughters for me the father of sons
wonder aloud "Why can there never be peace in the world?"
and I, being oh so clever
say, "Because the world does not exist, not as you mean it,
except as an oversimplified metaphor like string theory
in physics or the concept of time as vector and direction
in the movement of matter locked in the outward motion
of an ever-expanding universe.
How could there ever be such a thing save in the saying it might be so?"
And then, on this the morning after, I read a poem reminding me
how Vietnam vets described going home as—"going back to the world"
and glimpse in this American idiom, this lexicon of grunts
a confirmation to make me weep at hopelessness...
as if I almost understood the predicament of dreamers
falling asleep with books on our bellies
like big open-winged ravens
bringing the news of exhausted doves, of pax Romana a thousand years in
shadow flight above the veils of Visigoths
and riding the gentle and general thermals of eternal war

Failing Russian

as I sit in the rip of the flag next door
speaking of how things once were
with the wind in the flag
cracking its silk into storm
I think
the god of geese is a goose
and the god of gulls
a gull
and so, the Slovak lad
living on a small farm
at the edge of a Slavic village
refuses to learn Russian
from the squat woman with a man's moustache
teaching the language of oppression

when she turns her back to the class
he slips away
like a thief, he's off
through the window and out
beyond the sound of that room
like a map of Europe, burning

he goes home
to his Hungarian father
to his Magyar mother

he's hiding there
while Uncle Joe Stalin
who killed his daughter's squawking parrot
with a smoking pipe
who starved Ukraine
and murdered generals
is looking west
over ruined Stalingrad
where the frozen dead

lay littering the snow
like broken statues
shattered in ancient gardens of endless war

and the angry teacher
fails him
this lad who learns
seven other tongues with ease

and now the man
also remembers the day
he and his classmates scattered
across a collective farm
forced to dig potatoes
for the state

how he and a friend
ran away
foxing for freedom
at the field edge
skipping their duty
while flat forks turned dark earth
for edible stone
with the brown-starched flavour of grit
and the blindness that comes
to the hands
dull with work

and
there's a lesson in this

A Small Unquiet War

George lives in a quiet house on a quiet street
in a small and mostly quiet town
and he wants a quiet night of quiet sleep
but the midnight marauders come
the masked trash raiders come
with tiny supple hands, tiny pick-your-pocket hands of a child
the rat-faced marsupials come
the musky polecats come
hanging from the eaves, dancing down shingles
like pebbles let loose on the roof
come waddling up the boulevard
with the flag-tailed stink of hubris perfuming the fog
claw-raking the bark of the trunk coming down maple
coming down larch coming down from leaf-shadowed sky
rattling the entire star-dazzled world
hollow-thundering tin for corn, for
coagulated hog fat gumming a paper rag
for the last sweet lick
from a broken box, and so, one day
he'd had enough of their loud invasion
and thus began his small unquiet war
he live-trapped his first fat coon
and he carried her wagging her weight in the cage to the car
and she was fierce and fanged
and she fought the wire limits of her world
like the madness of a dark mind locked behind bars
and his sons feared her and refused
their father's work
and he caught and he caught and he caught
dimming the noise on the porch
though the sweet corn shivered its garden row
with a wild froufrou of gypsies in the wind
and he stopped at seventy-five, he stopped
twenty-five short of one hundred
he surrendered to the rodents

to the ravenous nut-hatching squirrels
he gave up and gave in
and he lives in a room
where he dreams
like a tree in the dark
for what is a man
but a tree in the dark without leaves

Opossum in the Barbecue

Were you waiting for us
standing alone on the grill
in the hollow darkness
of the cottage barbecue
feeding perhaps on the blackened fat
of former meals
so that when I removed the lightless hood
and lifted the lid
like the yawning mouth of a lazy beast—
there you were
real and rat-like
with a sudden bristling of startled fur
stuck out of the flesh
like much-used broom straw
browned by rain
and you blinked
and curled your lip on your sharp face
to show the teeth
and I leapt back
into the breath push
of my son's laughter
what was wild in me
flaring up, striking a match
in the dry tinder of my super-combustible heart
and you, what you thought of me
the big awkward ridiculous
energetic bird of my body
flapping backwards like a shot stork
as I met your gaze
like that of a thief caught in the kitchen
I took in then
at the moment of regained composure
that you were young
a half-grown possum child
out on a forage
perhaps for the first time

without mother
the warm-apron of her pouch
empty, dreaming
a hang-tailed dream
as you fall through the branches
of her bones
like the burn-weight of something blazing
as it drops through smoke

To Live the Day that Honours God
We Must Love the Dust We're Born From

In New York City
one restaurateur has hired for fashion and effect
un sommelier de l'eau
who from the rivers of the earth
who from beautiful bays, from freshets, from ancient springs
selects the best...
this water steward
in white short coat
with serious voice
is there to recommend
what complements the educated appetite.

Might I suggest
the glacial melt
of Auyuittuq from Summit Lake
near Overloard
where I have dipped my cup
to taste ten thousand arctic winters
at a sip

or what about the barn stream on the farm in late July
where Tom the hired hand leaned down
and placed his open mouth
about the pipe
and took the rusty gush
that bulged his cheek and made him gulp

or what about
Killarney lakes
where I have touched my hand
to water sky
and drunk the warm that floats me
belly blue
as if I'd swallowed heaven
 pool by pool
and might pull forth blue scarves of sky
to then amaze a room of children by

last night
my wife and I went walking
and it rained
to green the ground
while far away in Palestine
and far away in Hindu Kush
and far away in waves of war
where desert guns surround oasis wells
and weeping women drink their tears
we fill ourselves
with salt and dust
and mountain snows
that make us blind
as canvas bleached and shrunk and stretched beneath a brush
without the paint
last night
my wife and I went walking
and it rained
to green the ground
as humans whispering of the death
that is their own
might make just such a gentle sound

Look at That

yesterday at the dinner hour
while we picnicked on our cottage deck
three bikini-clad girls with a camera
were on the beach
striking provocative poses
on the sand
and at the water's edge
they arched their spines
and thrust their rumps up
for the lens
their long hair falling forward
their haunches
high, they rocked their hips
as two took turns
touching full length
thigh to thigh
flesh to flesh
as with the slow careful
movement of her kneeling
one set her pelvis
like a wishbone
on the tibia of the other
and glancing up at blue heaven
waited for the sky to respond

Observation Through a Wind-Stirred Tree

a young woman in pale summer skirt
and pearl-button blouse
sits in lotus, alone
on the beach
reading the morning news
fanned open
in her hands
like the wide span
of a paper-winged moth
meant for a kite
she folds it closed
and shifts, her body
in profile becomes
a broken W
her foot heels
pushing the sand
into sad hollows
like the small alms bowls
of the poor
her long hair
rusts in the sun
like wet iron
her mind it seems takes in the light
I watch her
through the fine-boned Y
of a sumac branch
stag-horned in the sun
those blood-crimson cones gored red
drop cool shade like imaginary gauze
darkening the green cleft
of the milkweed pod fecund with seed

what afterthoughts of water
we all are
though we warm the world
awhile
with the tracelines of our being
when our having been here
is of interest
and our having been gone
fills each word
when we're weak with failing breath

Slow Smoke

every day a seemingly-lonesome woman
walks the beach
her long grey skirts
drag gauzy shadows on the sand
like the drifting off of altar smoke
behind her
comes her sad old dog, nose down and
plodding in the frail aromas
of her having gone
when she lingers leaning for a shell
he stops as well
and pauses
enraptured
by a blur of dampened heat
he aches beside the lazy mirror of the surf
above some fragrant force, he's there to find
the perfume of a stone
a stinking stick
a sheepshead bone, dry weed
a castle's heaped erosion sagging on one side, a hand hole
seeping in the lag, a toe-marked trough
gull guano and a lover's name, half-vanished by an arrow heart
he laps the darkened blue
and waits
the much-considered moving on
he's mastered by
inconsequential tides in her
some ancient lupercal
the wolf of mind
has lost in ways the loss-lines
can't retrace
while empty wonder bores the moon
it fades

Again

I hear them on the beach
the morning girls, giggling
their beautiful bodies changing from within

again, it's summer
in the mind of spring
and something looms along
the dream ache of their growing bones
confuses every nerve with pleasure surfacing
like waves upon the moonlight-lifted lake

go now and choose your error
from an ancient tree of wrongs

in every generation
there's a willing force
surrendering the heart

Inside the Light

meditation on the hundred-year-old photograph "Bathing, Orchard Park, Port Dover, Canada"

a century ago
women wading in the lake
were photographed
in water to the waist
and otherwise beclad in black
like widows
weeded in their sorrow neck to knee
their skirts afloat
like morbid lilies mourning
all the drowned allusions to their gender
soaked in heavy fabric
to an over-laundered heart
their vestments caught the postcard
blue for blue
the double heaven of the day's daguerreotype
now there—below the sand
in silver marl and fractured shell
striations grip the digging child who seeps away
to touch the lifeless hand appearing through the deep
illusions of the heat of noon
this present summer strips us bare
our bodies naked to the sun
we'll dry into some future dream
when yet the mystery of who we are
is who we were, and when
we wear these bodies but a little while
we dress the flesh
in shadows of the age
and swim through vision's variations
of ourselves, resurfacing
like needles mending life to life
behold the handsome ghost
who cannot stir white linen with his breath
what value is the mist's damp mask
to him
he hides inside the light

Being Seen

young people
on the beach
are, it seems
striking poses

men flex
waxed pectorals
shining and gull-worshipped
gods of the looking-glass lake
with sand
on their soles
in the great wide sweep
of wind-worried time

and
open-legged women
lean down
laving their flesh in oil, the sun-browned
upside-down Y
of the body
filling itself
with a soft and obvious
swell of each breath
where the breasts both ripen and ease
ripen and ease
with the blush and retreat
of the shade

and oh, to be watched
as they aloe themselves
and go brown
along blue, or
to stand in the rocking of waves
in the tilting of chill
to be stained by the staining of foam
and to be lit by the watered-silk luminous cool
of a liquidy sky

how lovely they are
to themselves
how handsome and strong
how they long to be seen
as they fall
and are caught by the buoyant
reflection of *plunge*

like the heart of a sleeper in dream
we all of us slow
to one thought

to think
we are loved by the light

by the wind and the water in waves
by the sand set free
of our names

as we vanish in weathers of stone.

Let It Go

A tale from a Wednesday afternoon on the beach

the one group
let us call them 'the boxers'
for they were well-muscled, shirtless
stocky mesomorphs
wearing
the knee-length shorts
of sweet science

all afternoon till then
they had been standing on the beach
in a circle, turned inward
as if around a dying fire
and drinking
three young men and a girl
who was Queen Bee
of this purposeless cabal
and she had a hive in her belly
buzzing and rich with honey
and they were
droning on about drunkenness
and each of them
with a red glass in his right hand
using the other to crush the cans

and then onto this scene
the skateboarders came
a shambling, goofy, gangling
drifting-by crowd of them
skinny and feckless
looking skilled at nothing much
but the stand around and
the ride
and one of their crew
made a jest as he passed
by the boxers saying, "hey man, give me a beer …"

though mostly on their way elsewhere
the scrawny joker
hat on backwards
blond and sunburned
with ribs to count
and no hips to hold
his trousers up
went on his way as well, until

the muscled cluster, the trinity of men
who couldn't let it go
they started clucking
mock-talking about doing 'the chicken
walk' when the skater
turned back and said
"only jokin', man"

and he tried his best
which wasn't much
to keep on going

but these three men
five years his senior
kept up the henhouse
taunt until he finally turned again

and then
they walked — closing
up a new distance until
at the last in the gap-short between them
one boxer, one skater
chasing pride of fight
they ran at each other
like mountain rams
or Mexican roosters

the leaner guy
swung first
so his fist swooshed
as trees do in the wind
willow wise, poplar breathed
it is almost exactly so that larches snap their branches
in a little storm
and the boxer
came in under that swift enough whiffle of fist
and caught the skater
on the chin with a single crack
so he went down
like broken orchards
and then the victor finished
what he saw as his work
by kicking the kid in the face
so he went out cold
with a crimson grin

and this, it seemed
impressed many
for the good ones
came running to nurse the wounded
fellow, and the bad ones
gathered in high fives
hailed in heat to the coward's palm
and the circle of four
grew to six to eight
to ten to twelve
all vying to show their throats
to the moon
which is mostly only a lonesome stone
that must howl from here
to be heard.

The Children Come ...

like agents of accelerated time
the children come
to smash things
the tractor man had spared
upon the beach
he'd harrowed round and smoothed
the circumvented pyramid, the ziggurat
the sandy yurt
the small and vandalized idolatry of idle work
Ozymandias lost hours
in the architecting slave hands of the sun
these boys and girls
became the Visigoths of morning
running down
the cities of the gods
the sagging walls of Babylon
the golden mean
the compass of a broken light
the watered bricks
all tells of Troy
burned generations seven fathoms flat
and what
delightful ruin of Tulum
what joyful revel in the leveling
like fires of Gomorrah
floods of Gilgamesh
these pounding feet that thrilled
the heart
like horses in the breast of hills
imagine sad Pompey
the veil of ash
the rumours reaching Rome
the ululurum of that woeful news
the sudden victory of death
might contradict a kiss
or falsify a prayer

all oratory doom
to wake a dog to spirits
in the mist

and yet we build cathedrals
by the shore
and castle keeps
to watch the water
lap their dampness into dream

This Listening
 for Michelle

I was wearing my favourite T-shirt
the one that is priest-black
with the *Let it Be*   Beatles
on the front
and she said to me, finally
"now that I've known you
 for an hour
 I feel I can say this –
those guys ruined my world"

and she spoke
of how she was born
in an age
when she used to dress
in formal gowns
and go to dances
she talked of how she loved
to flow and spin and whirl
beneath a sparkling mirror ball

"after them
there was none of that
and I hated them for it
for the loss that comes
with change"

and for this listening
I learned

imagine my lake in the morning
how strange it is
without the evening moon
how sad the deeper light
how beautiful, how blue …

Imaginary Solitude

regard the pentimento of the world in fog
the graying blackness
of a distant line of trees
the fade of bluffs gone vague
as half-remembered hills adrift in mist
what water likes of rain
as gather-back and seep-away
and vanish-damp becomes
the undershadow of a darkened thought
the first regret
an error of the light
the brush sweep of a trailing cloud
gives rumour
of a shallowing to land
across the temporary blindness of the bay
when mind remembers
shores and wakes
this blush of chalky blue forgets
what humbles heaven
to this dull delight
this weather's worth of unseen loss
the wave that rocks the mast
to drench the sail
sets thinking at a cant
imaginary solitude cannot withhold

The Silver Lake Suite

Being Where We Are

we sit and we talk of rock-bottom rivers
the clean deep water
limpid to the very stone
you speak of the Moira
of your youth
how it meandered
threading through your family farm
holding the light
as a man dreams
his body abed
with a cracked-cream blind ticking
adrift in the dark forgetfulness of stars beyond stars
this remembering
that makes some muddy
with sleep
wakes what dwells
and silts alive at a willow bend
as shallow green
and the mind-filled lowing
of the soul
cows along the wind
in the breath of words

look from what we've lost
for being alive this long
to the new rain-fed stream
of your own name and story
in the foreground
is a man-made lake
doing turtle work
and you, my friend
are not sorry to be here.

Finding a Used Condom
on the Lynn River Trail

my fox terrier pup Sarge
sniffing the weeds grown green wild
along the trail
where we'd gone looking for water lilies
too late in the year
found and plucked and half-gulped
the phlegmy remains of a nearly filled rubber condom
which I, in fear of my dog choking to death on that second
far-less pleasurable peristalsis
thrust my fingers into his fiercely gobbling mouth
and drew it forth in one wet slobber
tossing it far away thinking "there, that is that"
and however repugnant, however ugly and raw
I'd saved him from gagging on latex
and the rheumy flavour of men

and so, on we went
down to the mud-gripped water
drawn into lazy flow
where the sky slept brown
like the pallid dreaming of an old man's nap
my mind haunted by the half-swallowed
appetite of my little dog
that pup hunger I'd interrupted with one contaminated hand
but I soon forgot and was mosquito busy in the shady hum of the Lynn
until upon turning around
that damned dog found what I had thrown
milkening into the shrubbery

and he was quick-gobbling
as if he'd been thinking of nothing else
only briefly though enthusiastically distracted by other things
such as
sparrow worry and cat spoor and the buzz and flurry
of a blue-winged damsel fly

and twice was more than enough
to rescue that bulbousity
which he was trying to dry swallow
as if he were following the serious instructions
of a gut god
and this were the most sacred sacrament
of all small dogs

but I gripped and pulled and flung
so it came snotting down
through sumac and skunk cabbage
like the milting ooze
of a wounded angel

how dare a poem contain
what overflows the language of hands

Thirteen Turtles

thirteen turtles
cling like limpets
to the dead-fallen driftwood
watching, it seems—themselves, reflected in
the still-water shadows
of Silver Lake, and morning—black-water blue
and bleary as an old barn window unwashed for years

and is there no fear
of numbers in them
not one pesky triskaidekaphobiac
among the baker's dozen
of dark-shelled dangers daring the
crack-thumb gods to action

do they not know
this is something so much like
the long-tabled reenactment
of the last supper

who will bless this crowd
which one betray
and which deny
old Leonardo paints the shell
black for black
and the marshy shallows wait

the mud-bottomed beauty
waits

as one head turns to the right
for that is all the work they'll do
this hour

that slow energy expended
exhausts them all

General Impression Size and Shape

when I was young in love
and my heart was fluttering
like a snared sparrow
caught in the green and quivering bone
of my breast
I was mind-blinded by desire
for the fruit and seed
of her conceiving
and my soul
was pure and white, oh
what a darkening
we wanted then

but today, while walking we startled
the living giss
of driftwood
standing as a come-to-life
bit of swamp branch
the great blue heron blinked
like a two-eyed limb
his body anchored by
graft of claw
a tree transformed or rather
half-transformed, for he was
fixed and water-twinned
by a double self beneath
a will-not-have-him unwinged sky

and has my heart not thus become
auk-ancient
in its tangled wilds

it flutters not
but beats great wings
as anxious angels do or autumn swans

my soul is grey
as fog-bound eggs
I live within that misty shell
like shoulders in a shirt
I am
half-born
exhausted
by an inner paradise
I take the wrong direction
toward the flight of death

Whooping Crane, Silver Lake

the local council
worries over the loss of the dam
where the lip
rots on the rim
of this man-made lake
the water falls
rushing from the slow shallows
that blacken the green
shores where what leans close
sees itself shining
in the turtle-pocked mirror
of a bird-blind sky

foaming under the cataract
the black creek flows
and spills and splits
real from reflected real
like a dream-masted yacht
in the dimming to true
of thought sails
and memory's hemp and
the heavy cloth
of a well-imagined storm

and the councilor says
'drain the lake
 to the mud
 and let us work...'

the neo-con says
'it's been drained before
 why not again ...'

and the men of action
put strong shoulders
to the sun
and burn their food
while the bottom cracks
into fissures
of elephant-fleshed clay
and belches amphibious bubbles
that break into spheres of milky light
either that, or
as happened yesterday
the endangered crane
will whoop
off the water
taking black-tipped
white-winged flight
amazing us all

The Turtle Mother

I saw her, so I thought, lost
and struggling half way up
a gravel hill she could not climb, she flayed
her legs upon the screed
like broken wings
I gripped her shell to help
and carried
the serious gravity
of her earth-brown bulk
and turned
towards the lake
as she came against her will
and craned her bullet head to see
who dared confuse her purpose in the world
and snapped her jaws
to breathe
a sharpened breath
that beaked the air
she hovered in
the watered leather of her flesh
clawed at the wind
with legs like living creatures caught
in a closed valise

my slow conviction through
the gorse like that of a water-bearing child
I flung her
so she spun and splashed
and sank
through surfaces
of sky and lake
and mud
each slower than the last

she plunged
and swam through murky swirls
and made her stubborn
startlement an ornament of tessellated life
come back to siege against
the cliff close by the shore

I thought
the moment satisfied
by ancient kindness
until
again upon the trail
I spied
the hole she'd dug
to house
her clutch of eggs
and almost wept
for what I'd surely killed
uncovered in the fox-faced sun
the lovely ovals of my ignorance
began to stink

Watching TV

I am standing
on the broken bridge
overlooking the lip of water
washing over the edge
of a shallow falls
where in that short height of the Silver Lake Lynn
the console
of a tossed-away television
lies sunken
in the slow rush, I am watching
its empty green vacant-glass reflection
wet with heaven
I am, as one might say,
watching tv
its prong and chord
thrust in the flow
like a stone-caught snake
essing with all
the black energy of something dying
something serpentine drowning
in the will of the water
and I
think of tear-washed paper
the unlacing of wet words
the loss of original ink
the dumbing off of sentient sorrow
the blurring to beauty of an over-sad hand
and how
one evening in a warm house
this imaginary window must have
bloomed blue and gone blank
like a dream startled away by the hissing of rain
and one awakening sleeper

as here
under the heavy
and radiant result of weather
it sat
silting backwards
unable to box itself over
the ridge
with all the purposeless inertia
of once purposeful things

it had perhaps
brought home both comedy
and war and had been
both loud with laughter
and quiet in the dark parlor of some
pine-scented orange-and-grey oleander
of Christmas
but here it has been locked
in the damp paralysis
of this relentless river
wanting only to plunge onward
through the ceaseless
urgency of the channel
out into the larger lake
but like a ghost under grass
like moonlit refractions of midnight
like oak shadow
and all the artlessness and otherness
of come-clear stars
dulled by streetlights
and dimmed by the glow of lived-in houses
I cannot
risk the brief illusion
of reified memory
on this stone-real desk
this poem might suffice
if the words weren't language
and the language
weren't breath

The Saddening Green
Inspired by a U.E.L. McQueen graveyard in Port Dover

Sometimes in the earth
there exists
such a saddening green
on a grave in the rain
with a sorrowful sun
gone grey as a shadow on stone
in the drab of the land
with the name on the stone
worn away
as it leans in the fading of moss
and is blackened
by lichening life
and the withering weather of spring

see how
they've sunk in the yard
these heroes of time
these tablets of yesterday's love
this oldening loss
this reverent vanish of bones
like the burning of branches to ash
a streak on the marl
or a mark on the sand
where the hand
holds death to its breast
or a face
wore the dust as a mask
as it slept in the language of prayer

who went on this journey
of souls
with the nesting of roots
through the mind
once kissed
with the fever of touch
once held
to the warming of dark
once dreamed
and remembered in youth
such a fathering mothering blue
from the promise of dawn
to the dimming of dusk
to the startling brilliance of stars
how the mystery comes
to us all
when we carry the light
like the lake, like the moon
like the well
too deep for the cup

Coneflower Meadow, Silver Lake, Summer 2010

there in the tall grass
the wild coneflowers stand on their stems with each bloom
like a brown-nosed pink-feathered
shuttlecock lost in the gorse, tossed
among green-white lace
and chicory-blue
challenging beauty to be
like the wide-eyed child of the poor
and they wave in the breeze
like the ruffle-necked dance
of a water bird
thrilled to be wading in weed
and they button the bodice of clowns
and they tighten the threads
of the earth to the earth
and they hold close
the closed and eternally lovely
presently unseen stars
each petal
a tooth from a comb of the sky
while the rumour
of honey goes large
in the hive
where summer light governs the buzz

Knowing My World

I want to know my world
how it drops before me this autumn
the green brain
of its fruit
let go
as a child lets go
his father, first his hand
in life, a high hand
he must raise his small arm
to reach, sapling-
thin and feckless
with water-pipe lean
and barely-muscled bone
that would green break
when struck hard to the earth
the ulna snapped
like an apple storm
when there's black sap in the peaches
and the worm coddles
and sours the pulp without wings
then, the son ages
at the white-fleshed
bedside of a dying man
whose large hand heaves heavy
as soaked wood floating
as it weakens on the pillowslip
and is veined
by the water-blue blood
of a slowing heart
entering the sweet secret
of that death-shared sleep
the blank dream
a graying over
like the oncoming of snow to the heavens
in cold weather

and I walk
the same familiar road near home
and notice
the hedge apples
gathering gravity at my feet
those Osage oranges
living high in the mother-tangled
atmosphere of the bow-wood tree
where they've swelled since August
gaining the stem-snap mass
of a doomed fecundity
gone rotten-brown on the ground

what a living fence they were
in Arkansas and Oklahoma and Missouri
but here, they roughen into tall nests
that shake the wind
all winter

I'm reminded of the cactus guards
in Cuba
that spiny hedge
keeping the calves from the cows
so we might
steal their milk
and starve the weaned get
bawling one lament
and surviving on stubble dust
their nostrils walked by flies

I'd name
every inch but this
for this
I weep, this knowledge
saddens the mortal soul
makes it wish away
all appetites
look, there's a time-hungry mirror
wants my tears

what a wet glass grieving!
what a dry-eyed man!

Strange Blueberries

In the Muddy Shoes of Morning

Last night in the dark
we walked mud-blind
crossing the sludgy roadwork
between house and car
and we seemed to find
in the unfrozen ground
of early spring
with every mucky step
the deep wet weight
of a puddleplace
or the clay-heavy suck
of something that wanted our shoes
and we clung together
laughing and yawing
and seeking a way
when earlier in the light
we had simply followed our eyes
over the sure dryness
of a mother-lucky path
but somehow
this sinking-in was far better
this sticky yellowing of shoe soles
feeling an almost toppling
and joyful giddiness
of shared fate
a commingling
as we sank and rose and pitched
like children
over the new-plowed furrows of a rain-soaked field

and I think now as I write this poem
of hundred-thousand-year-old preserved impressions
of a man and a woman
following the almost permanent footprints
to the very breath of their going
and their having gone

say this of me, reader
after the voice-vanish of this life
I felt the joy of foolishness
and in the muddy shoes of morning
saw love

Strange Blueberries

the Germans have a word
Schadenfreude
which means
laughing at the pain in others
and I wonder
as my friend tells
how he envies me
my good fortune
why it is
we are made this way

my baby grandson laughs
to see me
stub my toe
I wince   and want his youth
the new world he holds
that first delight
of blueberries
learning moonlight
the meaning of the bunch gall
of a goldenrod, I'll teach him that
and love without loss
the petty wisdom
of regret
the brief immortality
of almost eternal stars
what fevers in my spade
the voice of grass
to green his knees
a stone he might seek in the rain.

The Lengthening Ash

look to the stick
with its lengthening ash
its slow burn
its lonesome exhale
like your breath
in a word
that is new to the mind
from the radiant red
through the papery drooping of grey
what drops with a loss
like the dying of life
in the fall
breaks forth
with a lightening weight
when the faith
in a branch can't hold
where it works in the wind
grown fat on a graft

what a ghost womb we are
what a chaos of smoke
gone thin
like the fray at one end of a thread
where a child
licks the eye of this mend
and the man he's become
wears a hole in the heel
walking dream
to feel the spirit in thrill
at the vanish of drift
like the lack of the scent of the lake
gone far in on the land
in the fog-hold of morning
pulled wide
by lightest of winds growing old in the mist

what's a mystery then
in the touch of an eidelon hand
where pleasure's a breath
like the fanning of wings
in a hive working hard to hurry the heat from a wall

what's a hum of caress
but a blur
that confuses the soul
like a dry rose crushed in a book

Watching Purple Martins Glean Mayflies from the Wind

we wonder
does it matter
to anyone at all how they swoop—does it
matter to the web waft
of the spider
on the sill thickening her stitch
in the gap between glass and frame
or, to the vulpine evening
when in the gloaming
the wide-winged voluptuary
of a dimming hum
heals the silence
with a thinning
of sound like the slow closing of a music box lid
that lessening grey of a lessening grey
we feel with the wearing-out of worn-out darkness
in the early weave of day loss
at the knee-fold of night
such is the gauzy enervation of grace
the energetic fascination
of awe
when those who listen to the rain
slow down, or we who watch the foggening
plume of the mist, how it smoulders
over dips and valleys in dawn-water ponds
like the frothy gown
of some fainting-down dancer

for us
what happens
in the close-at-hand inches
occurs everywhere and revivifies delight

meanwhile my dying uncle
reaches out of the palings
of a bleached-white bone-sharpened being
and smiles
to touch my grandson's
little-fellow hand
over the chrome railing
of his final bed

and I see
how purple martins matter in this
how here
in that finger to finger moment
when young soul
and old soul
greet
breathing the same air
pulsing with one two-bodied heart
as the sand slims in the glass
with a double direction of drift
what is gone, what remains
like waking to or waning from
the unseen shadows of sleep

The Weakening

the tuck-winged gull
is dying in the sand
under the stony gravity
of a chalk-blue sky
come close enough
to feel the weight of weather
the pressing down and awful
slowness
of a solitary lonesome
knowing
greys the hour
in one grit-dusted eye turned upward
toward shadow-pass
what heart-blink
heavy darkness sees
as fade away
of seeming
is the light that burns the veil
within the veil
the large idea
of a cloud upon the mind
is pulled within
like breathing smoke
we vanish with
particulate of silence
to the quiet volume
of all vanity's regret

tomorrow he is gone
to join the energy
of broken life
he leaves behind
a feather drag of white
a bent and cantilevered wing
he cannot lift

two days ago
I saw him learning
final things

today I seek
to say the words
I do not know

I watch
the careful carelessness
of waves
that shape
the ever-changing presence
of an ever-changing shore
and there
the drift of feathers
and there
the onerous rag
the massy clump
the fractured span
this thing
the wind has thrown away

The Starving Man and I

the starving man and I
describe ourselves in bones
his soul
is like a windless flag
his heart's
a lingering of stone
in mud gone dry
when the river's low
without a thought of rain
his mind is fevered
and his words are few
he whispers heat
and sneers to smile
and wipes a gritty hand
against a buzzing mouth
the land he loved
is burning spring
and thirst regards a dusty well
that will not wet his tongue
what then am I
the pampered man to think
who with my belly full
my fingers greased with ink
I cannot count my ribs
I barely see my shoes
my soul is like a cloth
you pull from milk
the soaking white and gauzy luxury
of gibbous moon in mist
so full of light
the lake is lit for miles
my heart
swells on the branch
and plumply drums
of love
the spirit sweeps us both

for him a shroud
for me
a dance of veils
for him, a blurring glimpse
of darkness seen through fog
for me a blinding waft
of sleeper's sheets
I am become the dreamer in the dream

When the Light Returns

the thunder lay siege
on the lake all night
like the bellum of war
and I sat up for a while
watching
the concussive beauty of inconsistent darkness

and I thought of how
we had been
talking of Burma
and the bad news
coming from there
where monks are being murdered
and innocent citizens of Miramar
are being shot in the streets
and how
one man said of them
at hockey
"Yeah — too stupid to fight
       too stupid to get out of the fucking way!"

and that is how it is
with us
sometimes
to talk in coffee shops
to talk on hockey benches
to talk
in the long illness of human history
of how
we might simply
get out of the way
like what vanishes
when the light returns …

Heat Lightning

At sunfall
a weirdness
hung in the west
like mountains of evening
they clung to the lake
in ranges
and hovered over the pier
with the lighthouse sweeping the dark
and painting it greenovergreenovergreen
and then
the sky lay silent siege
on Erie
with a blush of luminous heat
and we here in the sound shadow
safety of home
watched the lovely involvement
of vapour and dust come to life

and then the next night
in the east
from over the trees
and the houses
the compass of lightning
swung round
and gave show
in the quiet illusion
of blinding the dark

and an old man
wondering what it was
his suddenly ancient amazement
that startles the stars
of the mind
and the moon of the bones
and the deep river blue
of the heart
to be still in the hush of his awe

as he says
'I have never seen this before'

Teaching My Dog to Read: The First Lesson

what we cannot see
with our eyes
hawks see
what we cannot hear
with our ears
owls hear
what we cannot smell
with our noses
dogs smell
what we cannot feel
with our flesh
butterflies feel
what we cannot taste
with our tongues
snakes taste
and this is the moon
in the womb
the stone at the centre of sleep
the red
that we draw from a dream
the ribbon of life
in the light of old tides
where what's deep
as a heart in the dark
with your palm to the bone of the breast
you might touch
what the hand
cannot hold.

Cozy

I am watching
the time-weakened dog
aching in road scraps
among dead leaves and broken branches
lying like unburied bones
on the road shoulder
where wet gravel
consumes the edge of everything
and we have all entered
the ochre ugliness of early spring
but he is hurting
old-in-the-hips
and limping along
the nose-faded earth
in the slow-houred loveliness
of a blue-lit morning
his heart like a fist in flannel
going dull-pulse dull-pulse
as he dreams
the rumour of squirrels
in the half-blind blur
of his health
and though I am here
close at hand
I am nothing to him
though I take him in
through this filter of sadness
and knowing
he shadows away
and is gone
where his body comes near
to the darkening darkness
and his breath
builds a dog out of dust

Remembering the Moment Yet to Come

sad-salted pavement of my winter thoughts
fit round delight
and rust the voice
to rattles
and the scrape
that scores pocked ice

the snow like rotted cloth
makes filth seem white
where recent cold
is sparrow-cruel

undress the windy weed with song
and shake brown seed
to seek the tattered harvest
of its lazy work
I find a candle's worth of words
like smoke slow-burned
on fire-damaged glass
within this looked-through glaze
though it corrupts seen things
and dulls
the language
to an unenduring grey
that will not bear
the walking weight
that shelters celebration
in a pregnant blue, and yet
this Christmas season
I'm refracted by an inner joy
where clarity
gives over to the loss of light
and story breathes new beauty
from a childhood church
where I recall the heat that says the door

and leaves a big book broken
onto Bethlehem
and midnight snows my father
through these words.

Pokeweed

When we bought a house in Brantford
the wealthy owner lied
and we lived in lie shadow
for seven years

until we sold
that big brick bent-windowed building
and moved and then moved and then moved again
now
we've settled
in a little cottage
near the lake
with a garden infested by pokeweed
we walk
on red seed staining the deck
by the door
and I look at the crimsoned boards
and think
of painted horses
thundering the wild plains
reddened by war
I think
of Lincoln's soldiers
writing home
their letters blood-brown
with words that follow the hand
the pen dipped in inkberry
telling the sorrows of loss
and the lonesome sadness
of being away
in Shiloh
at Bloody Pond
and wounded at Murfreesboro on Christmas Day
as my wife's father's mother's father
was injured that winter long ago in Tennessee
fighting the silence that comes
from forgetting

when the angel of history
sips what's boiled
and folds his storm-torn wings into darkness

my new neighbour
tells me that both
the leaves and the berries
of pokeweed are toxic to mammals
but not to birds

and I think of the lectin
that makes horses sick
and hogs mad

and curious babies die
for the hunger they feel
when reaching
for the blackened fruit
of a heavy branch
their fat little palms
with lifelines bruised by the world
their tiny mouths
blushed without breath.

Behold the Child of Time

Yesterday foul weather came
to rinse two fledglings from their nest
so they were washed away
and fell to grass
as featherless as plums, I found
their feckless bones
and unformed wings
stretched forth in fragile fails of flight
that drank the grey
and filthy breath of rain

the startled starling father
screamed alarm
the mother
fluttered at the fascia
like curling shards and snips of tin
torn loose to shake the startled soffit shade
aluminum dark-strawed with loss
what's gravity in this
the lure of water in the wind
the ugly hinges
of two big-mouthed beaks
stretched forth
and swallowed silence
that hungry quiet
like a gritty worm
the undulating gullet doomed
by soak of death

The Appetite's Result

The apple core I've left lying
upon the picnic table
must ring an aromatic silence
pulsing green
for the pismire wakes
a hundred yards away
and there
in the time it takes for me
to walk up the grade and back again
the brown pulp crawls
like a living spool
with thready legs
casting an ant line winding out
and flung loose
across the deck
to where it's sunk
a perfumed eye
hooking in a perforated hill
vermiculations following garden ground
floating in shallow grooves
like fine wire on brown water

What Falls On The Hill Doesn't Love Me

What falls on the hill
doesn't love me

I hear the branch crack
like a hen bone

and then
it lessens the green
breaks with shade

and lets itself go

A Stone on the Wind

The man stands
on the top step
of an unstable ladder
reaching up
over his head
on tiptoe
in the early middle of a winter day
the aluminum stride
unsteady on deck ice
skids and shivers
as he with his hatchet
sharp to the wood
limbs the tilting apple tree
lost to the flavour of snow
where branches claw shingles

and what solves gravity
what cantilevers
this fire crop
of disappointed song
what might have happened
to human bone brought low
for all its wingless worry he
did not
fall
he came home
ten fingers strong
two cold hands to the wheel
not broken
not fractured
but less   treed

In the Same Breath

We four were watching
from the vantage of a cottage deck
the great and only briefly
luminous incandescent
atmospheric light trail
in the over-arching blackness of a late night sky
with the close-at-hand milkspill of a pole lamp
lit to solve the shadowfear of a shaded hill
where a stringer stumbled
in stair fractions down the slope
and also the sand halo of a beach bulb
with its amber glow
and the gauzy buzz of mayfly clouds
humming in the heights
and also
the green swath
of a water beacon
and its crimson companion
each at the gull's end
of the dock channel
and also the moon
and the mist
but with each subsequent and eventual
startlement of meteor smudge
with its lambent trace of amazement
we woke just a little
as it is with touched dreamers
and all most ancient wonders
seeking the primal flavour
of first words
as birds hold singing
and in the same breath
silence.

I am a Work of Art   Do Not Touch Me

"Jesus saith unto her, Touch me not; for I am not yet ascended to my Father ..."
John 20:17   King James Bible

on the street in Port Dover
there stands a porcelain pig
painted nose-to-tail
in pastels of the town
it wears a paper saddle saying

> *"I am a work of art*
> *do not touch me"*

in Latin

> *'noli me Tangere'*

the Latin changed from Greek

> *'meta mon apton'*

meanwhile the bikers say aloud
about their hogs
with polished chrome
unto a passing crowd

> *"touch me*
> *—and I'll fuck you up!"*

Meditation on a Fly in Church

in church last week
I saw a bald man
with a housefly
resting on his
hairless scalp

meanwhile the homily
extolled a human Christ

Beelzebub, it seemed
was listening
from within the artful singularity
of a lonesome pest

I longed to swat
my neighbour's busy head

that tickled inch
of fragmentary swarm

the sermon's smallest ear

The Darkness Within

Learning the Dead Man's Float

for my cousin, Susan Scaman

A thousand years ago
when I was your skinny little cousin
with ribs you could count
when you were a big girl
and I was a small boy
I lay down
on the sky-washed blue
of our shared lake
with your hand on my heart
holding me up
in the great and buoyant beauty
of being
your calm voice stilling my thrash
for I thrashed like minnow
come alive on the waves
with the silver hurt of a shiny surf
I kicked at the excited thought of drowning
I refused to believe
in the tall-enough shallows
where, with my heartbeat
thumping your palm
like a bird wing held against bone
I flew as fear flies
and when you let go, I sank
and was lifted
as I sought bottom, sputtering

and for forty summers since
in all the out-too-deep hours
of faith loss and slow falling
through fathomless darkness
at the inbreath
of a mile deep ocean trench
whoever I am become
my mind in memory
keeps one indelible palm
like an ancient painted handprint
left on stone

The Darkness Within

when dandelions have gone
sagacious with summer
like little white-haired Einsteins of the wind

my son
drops his line
where the wood duck drifts
in easy circles

and the dropped hook seeks
the deeper presence
of a small plunge

I think
perhaps what is wisest
then, is not to think at all

but rather, simply
to let myself go
as light lets itself go
into darkness
which loves the light
in leaving

The Last Resting

I watch
where milkweed
rub the fence
in the summer
and see
how the orange-winged monarchs
arrive to ride
the nodding green
seed-rich pods
that split a ripening white
like time-cut women
and know
this is the last resting
before the long blue flight
the final hungering
before morning
and the first sun-powered dawn
where fearless
of the lake
they will rise
with wings like children blinking
on dust
what thoughts I have
of this
are briefly shadow-tattered
and soaked in darkness
all exhausted
beauty
pulsing its colour gone small
and far
into the borderless geography
of sky above water

A Rising Stillness

my milkweed
shapes its seedpod in the summer sun, hung lightly
from its stem
much like an old man's penny purse upon a cane of fence
where fragrance dies
and fades
into the green fecundity
so full of sticky kites
I know they'll split and burst and fly
white angels of a season
yet to come
and are we not alive enough to seek
or find
such future sands in us
the heart has its elixir
in the womb
the moon designs the daily tides
and pulls a secret thread
to shape a changing shore
I've seen
a stillness rising on the surface
like a sleeper's sigh
look there, a ship beyond the fog—it thrives in grey
like breath in words
or mind in someone else's ink
if you cannot thrill to this
the song inside the cherry tree behind the house
that hungers for sweet-sour red
and calls aloud to steal
the silence with its aviary appetite

I say this is my inner self
with wings, rose-bothered air
I buzz and crawl
and toddle on the verge
of some enripened thought
a gull grubs on the strand
as at a ghost worm of my soul
my spirit yearning at the world

whichever way I turn
a piece of glass I see
one glass, one world, one sky
one earth, one fine good darkness
yet to come
a rival to the temporary night
the apple shadow has my hand
I climb
to reach beyond my hand
and fall
to rise like windy shade that lifts
the darkness with the light

Flight School
during WWII the Turkey Point Marsh was used to train air-force bombers who dropped dummies and live bombs in the swamp

Out over the swale
in the marsh-shallows
of lake Erie near Turkey Point
where the tall weeds grow
I've come to the cliff to watch
monarchs float and land
their ovipositors open
to deposit life
on leaf edge
with all the larval promise
of late summer
where tiger-skinned worms
eat away at mortal darkness
as they thrive
and crawl and weave
wing homes

like phantom pilots in their greatcoats
high-collared in the cold
when over sixty years ago
with their shadows on the swamp
they flew here, dropping payloads
in the water
and learning about war
boys cut school to watch them
mere boys themselves
in their Harvards
hovering like angels
come from the lovely dangers of heaven

imagine Europe burning

imagine the urban infernos
of England, avenged
dream the dream flames
of Dresden and Berlin
the fire-licked windows
of the Reichstag, the stone swastika falling
and the final sneer
of the immolated Führer

I am here
swaddled in this cruel chrysalis
hunch winged
like a bird in a closed glove
wondering   am I the raven
          am I the dove

Ill Beauty

I am watching the little girl
snipping milkweed leaves
to feed the fat larvae
she has brought indoors
set in the deep prison
of a brown box ...
she holds in her hand
a clutch of green
a ragged bouquet of ugly
autumn withered old-veined things
a veritable gluttony
meant for the thickening of the worm
and she also insists upon
scissoring the chrysalis she finds
she has thread and glue
in the house meant for fastening
she will hang them all
like an elderly woman's chuchka
knickknacks from the orient
bric-a-bracs from the far east
imagine the weak-winged monarch
waking in the warm corrugation
of her urban bedroom
trying the windows
fluttering between sash and curtain hem
like wind-stirred price tags

I am reminded
of Marilyn Monroe—at her loveliest
suffering the light
as she sheltered her famous sorrow
the ill pulchritude of her woeful face
never more achingly gorgeous
than then

when she found herself
bound in the honey trap
of a failed marriage
weeping and begging to be left alone
as the cameras flashed
and she died into beauty
like a butterfly
high over the dream lake
of a little girl's counterpane
in the lonesome sunlight
of solitude and glory

Angel House

today
in the grey lattice-work
chiaroscuro of this sculptor's greenhouse
suspended
from weathered barnboard
in the inconsistent light
of early autumn
fastened like a tiny delicate
green oriental lantern made in miniature
ornamented by a band
of gold bead
the fettled chrysalis
of a monarch
and for the two of us
this was a first sighting
in the long life of aging men
a mutual blessing
better than the water
with its brilliant Zen-garden koi glittering
beneath the surface
better than the Osage
bow-wood branches bent into stone
this living moment
this ephemeral promise of wings
this invisible imago
angel house
of all blue whispers
we want this involute
infolding and sand-precious
single-grained instant we saw
the knowing thread
hanging from heaven
like the rust line of rain
that stains old lumber
below the oxidizing nail head
hammered in where the weather weeps
like a beautiful bride of the sky

Toward the Horses

In spring, the wind of dream
is moving
toward the horses—
there in blue surrender
a white drift
of easy mist
wings its way west
ghosting away like thought trails
of the dead
what clarifies the water completes the sky
like time that solves
a footplash in the rushing up
and silting down
of sand
I see in sunlit forsythia
and the photosynthesizing green
how the soul sees
how the heart sees
in the radiant blush
and the breath-on-glass
of the spirit in the flesh, I'm in
the old osmosis
of a gauzy milk-in-linen
mood and I'm
the world in thralls of being

I am the verdant push
the open palm, the one
that blooms in sleep to hear
the hooves within the hill
sound out the hollows of touch
like the living heart of the land
where what caressing gives
the hand receives
the resonant bone of talk
like darkness on the edge of light
surrounds the language
of the living drum we are
in silent beauty and in quiet
grace—what hears is heard
what speaks becomes the vessel
of a fuller phrase
oh there, toward the horses
farther than the farthering of farthest stars
the mind lies darkening with dawn

Vantage

"The absent tree has now become a vantage point."
    Alberto Manguel

I start to climb the loss, see there,
I set my foot
where darkness fails to fall, it lifts
the vanished leaf against the light
the nothing apple rusted russet in the sun
the coddle wing
that moths about the failing fragrance
of a shadeless shade
I grip at ghosts
and rise like mist in heat
where memory sets heaven
in a bowl of bone—to dream
the morning moon upon the lake is more
and yet
I hold with lessening, I'm fevered
with the feckless ailment of recall
I'm fathered by frail eidolons
made real
and maiden born and spirit crowned
in monumental vapors
like a stone enveiled in fog
old appetites of time
the satiated and eternal past
has passed away in this
unthirsting thing
the roots remain to foil
the shovel face
the broken trunk becomes
a saw-grass vase
the heartwood chokes on sand
the rising dune reclaiming as the wave reclaims its foam

I feel my dust in this encollaring
the hand drift
of a dark caress
the word beyond the sound of words
the limits of a sentient breath
the wind that moves the weather
through the world
it seeks the leaf to shake
green volumes of its living voice
but where the voiceless stoma curl
to palm the dryness of the rain
suspended in the up draw
of a traceless blue
I find the whispering refusal to be gone
and take my nutriment from that
and lean my ladder
on the evening and the dawn

Previouisly published by
Hidden Brook Press

Island on the Wind-Breathed Edge of the Sea
ISBN – 978-1-897475-19-5
www.HiddenBrookPress.com

Sweet Cuba
The Building of a Poetic Tradition: 1608-1958

Translators: John B. Lee, Dr. Manuel de Jesús Velázquez León

ISBN 978-1-897475-53-9

A Note About the Author

For poet, John B. Lee, 2010 has been something of a banner year. Named recipient of the International Poets Academy Lifetime Achievement Award for Global Peace through World Poetry, he also received the distinction of being presented with the Award of Merit for Professional Achievement in Poetry from his alma mater, the University of Western Ontario. In addition to these two honours, he received the Golden Chapbook Award, the Rubicon Press Winter Chapbook Award, the Cranberry Tree Press Award for Poetry, and he was short-listed for the Vallum Poetry Award. With the publication of Sweet Cuba: The Building of a Poetic Tradition 1608-1958 in the summer of 2010, he and his colaborator and co-translator, Dr. Manuel de Jesus Velazquez Leon, have produced an impressive bilingual anthology that has been called "the most significant book of translated Cuban poetry ever published." In 2005 he was named Poet Laureate of Brantford in perpetuity and in 2010 he was named Poet Laureate of Norfolk County. *In the Muddy Shoes of Morning* is the third part of *The Port Dover Trilogy*. Part One, *How Beautiful We Are,* won the inaugural University of Windsor Souwesto/ Orison Award. Part Two, *The Place That We Keep After Leaving*, was short-listed for the same award. Now with the publication of *In the Muddy Shoes of Morning*, John B. Lee returns for inspiration to the place he calls home, Port Dover, a fishing community on the south coast of Lake Erie, deep in his beloved Souwesto, where in the closing words of his title poem he writes–

> say this of me, reader
> after the voice-vanish of this life
> I felt the joy of foolishness
> and in the muddy shoes of morning
> saw love

www.ingramcontent.com/pod-product-compliance
Lightning Source LLC
Chambersburg PA
CBHW021115080526
44587CB00010B/529